970.3 Nez Perce
The Nez Perce of the Pacific
Northwest

W9-CFV-621

WE WERE HERE FIRST
THE NATIVE AMERICANS

THE
NEZ PERCE
OF THE PACIFIC NORTHWEST

Earle Rice Jr.

PURPLE TOAD
PUBLISHING

P.O. Box 631
Kennett Square, Pennsylvania 19348
www.purpletoadpublishing.com

WE WERE HERE FIRST
THE NATIVE AMERICANS

The Apache of the Southwest
The Inuit of the Arctic
The Iroquois of the Northeast
The Nez Perce of the Pacific Northwest
The Sioux of the Great Northern Plains

Printing   1   2   3   4   5   6   7   8   9

Publisher's Cataloging-in-Publication Data
Rice, Earle
   The Nez Perce / Earle Rice, Jr.
      p. cm.—(We were here first. The Native
Americans)
   Includes bibliographic references and index.
      ISBN: 978-1-62469-077-8 (library bound)
   1. Nez Perce Indians—Juvenile literature.   I.
Title.
                                    E99.N5 2013
                         979.5004974124—dc23
                                      2013946336

eBook ISBN: 9781624690785

Printed by Lake Book Manufacturing, Chicago, IL

CONTENTS

This Nez Perce warrior strikes a classic pose on horseback. The Nez Perce were superb horsemen and fought with uncommon ferocity when provoked.

CHAPTER 1
INCIDENT AT WHITE BIRD CANYON: A BRIEF HISTORY

The hearts of White Bird's band of Nez Perce Lamtamas were heavy in early June 1877. Their way of life was changing forever. The white authority had ordered them onto a reservation. All the Nez Perce bands had gathered at nearby Tolo Lake, in the Idaho Territory, for one last celebration of the old ways. There was dancing and feasting and the harvesting and drying of camas roots. The ritual featured a parade of warriors on horseback. They rode in a large circle around the camp.

One rider stood out from the rest. His name was Wahlitas, or Shore Crossing. He rode in the rear of the procession. It was a place of honor, reserved for only the bravest of the brave. Shore Crossing was a fine warrior and athlete, powerful yet mild tempered and charitable. While prancing about, his horse accidentally trampled one woman's spread of drying camas roots. Yellow Grizzly Bear, her husband, yelled angrily at Shore Crossing: "See what you do. Playing brave you ride over my woman's hard-worked food. If you are so brave, why not go kill the white man who killed your father?"[1]

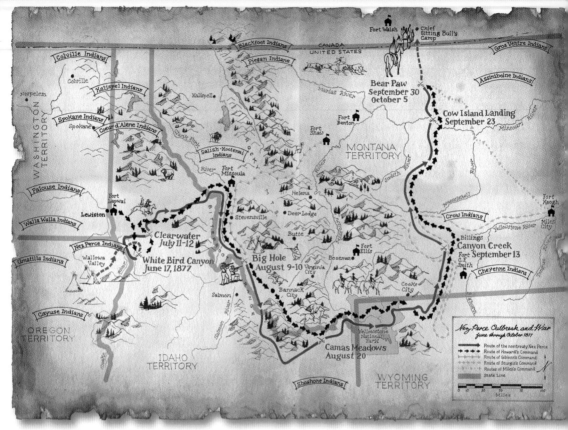

Hostile Indian action at White Bird Canyon started the Nez Perce War of 1877. The Nez Perce fought a 1,700-mile running battle across four states before surrendering to U. S. Army troops at Bear Paw.

Three years earlier, an old miner named Lawrence Ott had become involved in a land dispute with Shore Crossing's father, Eagle Robe. Ott pulled a revolver and shot him in front of four Indian witnesses. Eagle Robe died a slow death over several days. As he lay dying he sent a message to his son, Shore Crossing: "Tell him for my sake, and for the sake of his brothers and sisters, and in fact for the whole Nez Perce nation, to hold his temper . . . and not wage war on the whites."[2]

Later, the local Indian agent brought Ott and the four Indian witnesses before a grand jury. But the four witnesses refused to swear an oath to the white man's God during the swearing-in process. As a result, the jury declined to hear their testimony and set Ott free on a plea of self-defense. Shore Crossing, despite his rage, honored his father's dying wish. He did not follow the Indian tradition of drawing blood for blood. After Shore Crossing had held his fury in check for three years, however, Yellow Grizzly Bear's taunt finally unleashed an uncontrollable urge for vengeance in the young warrior's heart.

On the morning of June 13, Shore Crossing called on two cousins, Red Moccasin Tops and Swan Necklace, for help. The three young warriors painted their faces and rode down White Bird Hill to the Salmon River in search of Lawrence Ott—and revenge. They found Ott's farm deserted. Anticipating a possible Indian raid, he had gone into hiding. The three avengers rode up White Bird Canyon in search of alternate targets. Fueled by firewater, they found and killed four other settlers unfriendly to White Bird's Lamtama band and wounded a fifth.

White Bird Canyon was the site of the first battle between the Nez Perce and U. S. Army troops under General Oliver O. Howard in June 1877.

Shore Crossing and his cousins continued their rampage for three days. Seventeen braves joined them, one from Chief Joseph's Wallowa band, the rest from White Bird's Lamtamas. When their killing spree ended on June 15, fifteen more settlers lay dead, including women and children. Hair Combed Over Eyes, a leading Lamtama warrior, said later, "The warriors, crazed with drink, mistreated and killed a few women and children. This should not have been done."[3] But it was done—and war between the Nez Perce and the white man's soldiers loomed certain and imminent.

Members of the Nez Perce nation call themselves Nee-Me-Poo (nee-MEE-poo). In their language, the name means "the real people," or simply "the people." The Nee-Me-Poo cherish their homelands on the Columbian Plateau. They believe they have occupied the land since the world was first populated. Archaeological evidence traces their presence there as far back as thirteen thousand years. Their first contact with white men came in 1805. They gave shelter to explorers Meriwether Lewis and William Clark and helped them down the Columbia River.

Lewis and Clark called the Indians Chopunnish. Clark described them as "stout, portly, well-looking men; the women are small, with good features and generally handsome, though the complexion of both sexes

This artful sculpture by Nez Perce descendant, Doug Hyde, depicts Chief Twisted Hair directing Meriwether Lewis (left) and William Clark (right) to the perilous westward waterway to the Pacific Ocean.

A Flathead family poses in front of their teepee. They were the easternmost tribe of the Plateau Indians. They did not practice head-flattening, but some of their slaves did.

is darker than that of the Tushepaws [Flatheads]."[4] French-Canadian fur traders arrived later. They gave the Indians the name of Nez Perce, meaning, "pierced noses." (In English, the name is pronounced *NEZ PURSE;* in French, *NAY per-SAY.*) Though a few Nez Perce wore nose pendants, most did not. Nevertheless, the name stuck.

British Canadians came after the French, followed by American missionaries. The Nez Perce welcomed the newcomers and extended their friendship. Change came to the northwestern plateau at a startling pace. Pressures from new diseases, new trade relations, Christian missionaries, and the politics of America's expansionism began to overwhelm the simple Nez Perce way of life. Some bands allied themselves with missionaries; others with dishonest traders or land-hungry settlers. Still others intermarried with fur traders, who introduced them to tools, blankets, and guns. Outside forces gradually undermined Nez Perce unity.

In 1855, at the Walla Walla Council, Isaac I. Stevens, the governor of Washington Territory, created a 7.5-million-acre reservation for the Nez Perce. A few tribal leaders agreed to exchange some of their land for

In this painting, artist Gustav Sohon depicts the arrival of the Nez Perce Indians at the Walla Walla Treaty Council in May 1855. The treaty created a 7.5-million-acre reservation for the Nez Perce.

settlement. In return, they would retain the rest of their land and receive the protection of the reservation, along with money, schools, livestock, and tools. Other Nez Perce leaders rejected the treaty and refused to be bound by a paper agreement.

Between 1863 and 1877, disunity increased steadily among the tribal bands who accepted the reservation and those that did not. Common cause finally reunited them in the spring of 1877, when a band of young Nez Perce warriors rode off into White Bird Canyon on a reckless killing spree. A detachment of cavalry from Fort Lapwai answered quickly—and seventy years of peace between the Nez Perce and whites exploded into violence.

Unkept Promises

The Walla Walla Council of 1855 was held in the Walla Walla Valley at a site called Waiilatpu, or Place of the Rye Grass. Isaac I. Stevens held the meeting on May 29. His orders were to gain title to tribal lands in the Washington Territory. The land would be opened for white settlement.

Chiefs at dinner, Walla Walla Council

In return for the rights to much of their lands, Stevens offered the tribes reservations, cash, and the right to keep their traditional hunting and fishing grounds. The first treaty with the Nez Perce was concluded on June 11, 1855. It established a 7.5-million-acre reservation for them that excluded non-Indians.

The exclusion did not last long. In 1860, gold was discovered along the Clearwater River. Prospectors, miners, and speculators descended upon the Indian lands in droves. Settlers and merchants followed, and many government promises went unfulfilled. The government proposed a new treaty in 1863. It slashed the Nez Perce reservation to 746,651 acres—less than one-tenth the original promise. Only a few chiefs signed the treaty. Resisters included Chief Joseph of the Wallowas and Chief White Bird of the Lamtamas.

President Ulysses S. Grant, as part of his peace plan, issued an executive order in 1873. It added a tract of land in the Wallowa Valley to the reduced Nez Perce reservation. When non-Indians continued to settle in the area, however, Grant yielded to their pressure. He reversed his order in 1876, in another of many unkept government promises.

Nez Perce society was built around large families like this one. Young men and women usually married by the age of fourteen. Brides were often purchased, and polygamy was common.

CHAPTER 2
ONE WITH THE EARTH: THE LAND AND ITS PEOPLE

The Nez Perce think of themselves as being one with the earth. "The earth is part of my body. I belong to the land out of which I came. The earth is my mother."[1] So said old Toolhoolhoolzote, leader and shaman (medicine man) of the nontreaty Pikunan band of Nez Perce. In those simple words, spoken more than a century ago, he expressed the timeless and inseparable connection he and his people felt—and still feel—to the earth. Nez Perce regard the earth as the mother of all living things. They revere it and believe a supreme spirit willed them to live in a certain area.

The Nez Perce homeland was in a region that covers what are now northeastern and central Oregon, and southeastern Washington. It was centered in the area of the Snake and Salmon rivers. Both rivers are tributaries of the Columbia River to the north. The Columbia drains the high plateau country between the Rocky Mountains to the east and the Cascade Mountains to the west, and flows to the Pacific Ocean. This diverse and spectacularly beautiful region covers an area of about 11,000 square miles. Tribes of this northwestern area are part of the broader Plateau Culture.

The Nez Perce represent the largest and most important tribe of the Sahaptin-speaking subgroup of the Plateau

Penutian language family. At the turn of the nineteenth century, the Nez Perce numbered about six thousand people. They lived the partially nomadic life of hunters and gathers. "A ceaseless quest for food ordered the life of the Nez Perce," notes western historian Robert M. Utley. "They planted no crops but moved about to where food could be had."[2] Following a seasonal round, they moved from the rivers, where they fished for salmon, to the forests and meadows, where they hunted game and gathered wild plants.

Salmon and roots of the camas (an onion-like plant of the lily family) were the staples of their diet. Men fished with snares and nets, and hunted with spears, bows and arrows, and later, guns. Available large game included deer, elk, mountain sheep, and bear. Small game consisted mostly of rabbits and grouse (large bird) caught with snares. When they acquired horses in the early eighteenth century, the Nez Perce extended their hunting grounds to the Great Plains to hunt buffalo (or bison). Women dug for camas and other roots, and gathered fruits, nuts, and seeds to add to their diet.

Because of their transitory lifestyle, Nez Perce lived in two kinds of houses—earth or pit houses and tepees (tipis). They built a more permanent winter earth or pit house by digging a large pit and covering it with earth, cedar bark, and woven mats of plant fibers laid over a pole framework. Oval-shaped earth houses sometimes extended to a hundred or more feet in length and housed several families. Single families lived in smaller, round earth houses. During summer fishing and hunting trips, Nez Perce lived in easily movable, cone-shaped, hide-covered tepees patterned after those used by Indians of the Great Plains.

Before they acquired horses in the eighteenth century, Nez Perce traveled either on foot or in canoes. They later adopted horse- or dog-drawn travois from the Plains Indians for transporting loads. A travois consists of two trailing poles that carry a platform or net for the load. Nez Perce warriors became skilled horsemen and horse breeders, particularly noted for developing the Appaloosa.

Nez Perce women fashioned most of their family's clothes, primarily from cedar bark and animal skins. Above is an elk-hide shirt with deer-hide fringes. Porcupine quills were used to decorate it.

Nez Perce fashioned their clothing primarily from cedar bark and animal skins, such as deerskin, mountain-goat skin, and rabbit skin. Men typically wore long, fringed buckskin shirts, thigh-length leggings, belts, a breech cloth, and moccasins. Women wore long, belted buckskin dresses, knee-length moccasins, and handsome basket hats woven from bear grass and cornhusks. Men's shirts and women's dresses were often decorated with beads and traditional ornaments. On special occasions, men wore headdresses made of a ring of feathers that stood up from a headband. Bison-skin robes provided additional warmth in the winter.

As in most cultures, Nez Perce men, women, and children had specific roles to play. Men served as hunters and warriors. They were responsible for feeding and defending their families. Women covered homemaking responsibilities—cooking and cleaning and making most of the clothing and tools their families needed. Both men and women took part in storytelling, artwork, music, dancing, and natural medicine. Children helped with family chores, but learning to become responsible adults

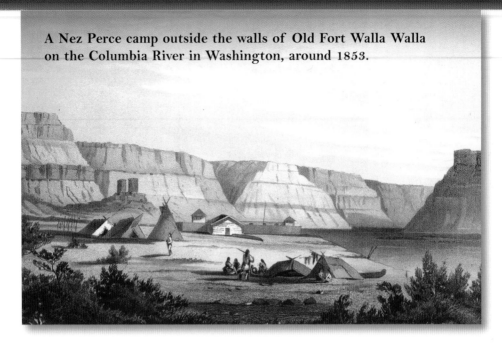

A Nez Perce camp outside the walls of Old Fort Walla Walla on the Columbia River in Washington, around 1853.

was their main duty. Like all kids, they had dolls, toys, and games to play with—after their work was done.

"Communities clustered around families and extended kin groups and linked together into bands identified with specific river drainages," writes Nez Perce historian Allen Slickpoo. "Some leaders organized groups to engage in hunting, others specialized in warfare, and still others focused on religious rituals, conflict resolution, or healing."[3] Each village or band had a headman and ruled itself. Tribal structure consisted of a loose federation of bands that was governed by several chiefs or headmen.

Overall, the Nez Perce were peaceful. They enjoyed friendly relations with their neighbors—the Cayuse, Yakima, Walla Walla, Umatilla, Kalispel, Spokane, and Coeur d'Alene in the north and west; and the Flatheads in the east. When aroused, however, they were second to no one in a fight. Their enemies—the Shoshone and related Paiute bands in the south; and the Sioux, when they crossed the Plains on seasonal hunting trips—occasionally felt the Nez Perce fury.

In times of conflict and strife, Nez Perce warriors took comfort in knowing their *wyakin* (guardian spirit) would protect them.

Abundance of Appaloosas

Early in the eighteenth century, around 1730, the Nez Perce acquired horses. "Paiutes and Shoshonis, the most constant enemies of the Nez Perce, except at trading fairs, rode up from the northern part of the Great Basin with horses and slaves they had captured during their raids,"[4] writes historian David Lavender. Horses changed the Nez Perce way of life forever.

Nez Perce war chief on horseback

About 65 million years ago, when volcanic eruptions were still forming the Rocky Mountains, horses and other animals perished from North America. Anthropologists generally agree that Spanish explorers reintroduced the horse to the continent in the early sixteenth century. Conquistador Hernán Cortés is known to have brought sixteen horses to Mexico with him in 1519. From Mexico, horses spread to the southwestern United States, the Great Plains, and points northward.

American explorer Meriwether Lewis commented on the high quality of Nez Perce horses in his journal entry on February 16, 1806: "Their horses appear to be of an excellent race; they are lofty [elegantly] formed active and durable; in short many of them look like the fine English coarsers [coursers: swift, valuable racehorses] and would make a figure in any country."[5] Those horses have come to be known as Appaloosas.

"The size of the Nez Perce herds ballooned fantastically," adds author David Lavender, "especially in the Wallowa country."[6] In 1870, a herd as large as 10,000 head was sighted in a single meadow on the Wallowa Plateau. The Nez Perce became excellent riders, horse breeders, and trainers.

The Indian trickster, Coyote, took his name from the American coyote shown here. Tricksters could be cunning, like the coyote, or funny, and sometimes both.

CHAPTER 3
RELIGION, SPIRITS, AND STORIES

"Living in intimate and precarious equilibrium [careful balance] with the environment, the Nez Perce pursued a spiritual life given form by nature and the individual's relations with nature," writes author Robert M. Utley. "The land, especially their homeland, compelled a worshipful, mystical veneration."[1] The Nez Perce believed all living things have spirits, possessed of powerful and mysterious qualities. They extended these qualities to many natural phenomena and ritually significant places. The Nez Perce also felt a deep connection with inanimate elements that shared their living space. Even rocks and trees held special powers. Their spiritual relationship with nature reaches back eons to their beginnings.

The Nez Perce traced their origins to the Indian trickster-figure, Coyote. Legend holds that Coyote entered the belly of a beast that was devouring all the animals on Earth. He cut a hole in the monster's ribs, and all the animals escaped. Coyote then cut up the monster's heart and scattered the pieces to the four winds—North, South, East, and West. Wherever the pieces landed, a tribe was born. In this way, the Nez Perce came to be.

Almost all Nez Perce sought the help of a guardian spirit called a *wyakin* to maintain a personal link to nature. A *wyakin*—in the form of a hawk, a rock, lightning, a wind, or other natural

Nez Perce boys and girls would seek a personal *wyakin* in an isolated place at the age of puberty. The *wyakin*—or guardian spirit—might take the form of a hawk, rock, lightning, wind, or another natural entity.

form—provided a source of power to its owner for protection and assistance along the pathway of life. Nez Perce children between the ages of nine and twelve, both boys and girls, were sent out alone on a Spirit Search to some mystic site—a cave, a lake, a mountain—to seek their own *wyakin*. They brought no food or weapons with them and only a few sips of water. For as many as five days and nights, they fasted and prayed. Usually a *wyakin* would appear to the seeker in a dreamlike vision, or as a material thing, such as an animal or flash of lightning—and sometimes not.

"Lightning storms, animal howls, mysterious night creakings, or imagined footsteps sent some scampering back to the village in fright," notes David Lavender. "Others simply grew homesick."[2] Those who

Lightning is one of many natural phenomena chosen as a guardian spirit by Nez Perce youth.

returned without a *wyakin* could try again on another quest. They could also receive a *wyakin* as a gift from a family member. "If that recourse did not work, the unfortunate seeker was doomed to an undistinguished career, perhaps even to poverty."[3]

The *wyakin* and other spirits formed the basis of many important rituals practiced by the Nez Perce. In a winter festival known as the Guardian Spirit Dance, or *Wee'kwetset,* young people who had recently found their spirit would take turns dancing and singing in front of everyone. While dancing, they would reveal their guardian spirit for the first time by singing their spirit song. A shaman often convened this ritual, which represented one of the main religious ceremonies of the early Nez Perce.

Rituals played a large part in their spiritual life. At life's beginning, they observed birth and naming rituals; at its passing, they honored the deceased with another ritual.

The Nez Perce never made fun of misshapen humans or animals lest their ridicule cause similar flaws in babies. For good luck, Nez Perce sewed the umbilical cord of a newborn baby into a small pouch and attached it to the baby's cradle. Tribal members held a special ceremony to name a child and honor it with gifts. They often named a child after a notable ancestor in the belief the child would take on similar qualities.

A Nez Perce death ritual began immediately with the wailing of females close to the deceased. Attendants painted the face of the deceased red, washed and dressed the body in new clothes, and wrapped it in a robe for burial the next day. They placed many of the deceased's valuables in a grave, and perhaps sacrificed a favorite horse and left it close by. A shaman performed the rituals needed to ensure against the return of the deceased's ghost, while attendants ritually purified

Nez Perce women wore their hair loose or in two braids (shown wrapped here). Unlike this woman, most Nez Perce did not wear nose rings.

This gleaming bronze sculpture of Mother Earth in Lewiston, Idaho, stands as a symbolic reminder to Nez Perce of their eternal link with nature.

themselves. The surviving spouse entered into a year of mourning, after which he or she was permitted to remarry.

The Nez Perce honored the Hanyawat, or Creator, and Mother Earth through special songs and dances. Some tribal members embraced Christianity, but most practiced a spirit-based religion of some sort. One such religion is the Dreamer (or Seven Drums) Religion, founded by the Wanapam prophet Smohalla (1815–1895). It is also known as the Prophet Dance, the Washani Religion, and other names. Smohalla claimed that visions came to him in dreams, and that he had experienced death and returned to life with important messages for the living.

"Men who work cannot dream," declared Smohalla, "and wisdom comes to us in dreams."[4] His religious ideas, summed up in the Washani (Dancer's) Creed, advocated resisting the ways of the white man and returning to the natural unity between the people and the earth.

Some scholars consider the Nez Perce Prophet Dance to be the forerunner to the circular Ghost Dance (shown here). The Ghost Dance originated in the Walker River Reservation in Nevada in the 1870s.

"[W]hen God is ready, he will drive away all the people except the people who have obeyed the laws [Creed]."[5] Smohalla's philosophy combined elements of Christianity and native beliefs, but it rejected the culture of white Americans.

Nez Perce performed a traditional Prophet (Washani) Dance using seven drums, seven singers, and several brass bells. Both men and women used eagle and swan feathers to symbolize flight from Earth to Heaven. Some scholars refer to the dance as the forerunner of the Ghost Dance, a circular dance made famous by the Sioux at Wounded Knee. Both dances encouraged resisting the white man's ways, but the Prophet Dance was less aggressive than the Ghost Dance—but only to a point.

First Missionaries

The Lewis and Clark expedition, known as the Corps of Discovery, opened the American Northwest to white adventurers in 1805. Protestant missionaries brought Christianity to the region in 1836. Catholic missionaries arrived four years later.

Presbyterian missionaries Henry Harmon Spaulding and his wife, Eliza Hart Spaulding, headed west in 1836. They traveled in the company of fellow Presbyterian missionaries Marcus and Narcissa Prentice Whitman. Eliza and Narcissa became the first white women to cross the Rocky Mountains. The Spauldings settled among the Nez Perce at

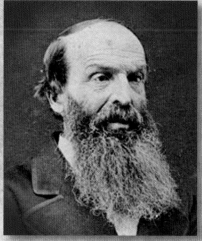

Henry Harmon Spaulding

Lapwai, near Lewiston, Idaho; the Whitmans, among the Cayuse at Waiilatpu, in the Walla Walla Valley. They built missions at their respective locales and began providing religious and educational services.

The Spauldings started agricultural programs and taught classes. Henry later obtained a printing press and published the Gospel of Matthew and other works in the Nez Perce language. The Whitmans likewise preached the word of the white man's God among the Cayuse. Marcus, who was a physician, also ministered to their medical needs.

In 1847, a measles epidemic killed half of the Cayuse tribe. Some tribal members blamed the deaths on the Whitmans. On November 29, 1847, a raiding party of Cayuse killed the Whitmans and twelve others. The killings became known as the Whitman Massacre. Oregon officials declared all Cayuse lands forfeit. They later opened them to homesteading without regard to Native American title. Missionary authorities closed the missions in the region, and white settlers waged a short-lived war against the Cayuse.

Chief Joseph was one of those rare men born to do great things. When he spoke, men listened. His Nez Perce name was Thunder Rolling in the Mountains.

CHAPTER 4
CHIEF JOSEPH AND THE LONG FLIGHT

After their first meeting with Lewis and Clark in 1805, the Nez Perce kept the peace with white men for 70 years. But a continuing stream of white settlers poured into the Northwest. By 1876, the nontreaty Nez Perce had to move onto the reservation.

In May 1877, Chief Joseph and other Nez Perce chiefs met with General Oliver O. Howard at Fort Lapwai, the reservation headquarters. Howard, a one-armed Civil War veteran, headed the government's negotiating committee. His job was to persuade Nez Perce leaders to vacate their lands in return for goods and money.

On May 15, after the talks had dragged on for days without resolution, Howard lost his patience. He ordered the nontreaty Nez Perce onto the reservation within 30 days or face military action. Joseph and his fellow chiefs finally yielded to his demands and began preparations to move onto the reservation. Two days before time ran out on Howard's ultimatum, the incident at White Bird Canyon occurred. Everything changed.

Chief Joseph knew Howard would send soldiers after the nontreaty bands to avenge the slaying of white settlers.

"I would have given my own life if I could have undone the killing of white men by my people,"[1] he said later. Joseph opposed war, but he now felt committed to supporting White Bird and his people. He joined them at their camp in White Bird Canyon.

Meanwhile, General Howard had dispatched a 100-man detachment of cavalry-infantry out of Fort Lapwai to intercept the rebellious Indians. He placed Captain David Perry in command of the detachment, saying, "You must not get whipped."[2]

Perry replied cavalierly, "There is no danger of that, sir."[3]

At dawn on June 17, 1877, Perry's detachment arrived at White Bird Canyon. A party of six Nez Perce approached them under a flag of truce, hoping to find some way to avoid further violence. The inexperienced soldiers were having none of that and opened fire. The Nez Perce returned fire. When the shooting ended, one officer and thirty-three enlisted men lay dead—one-third of Perry's command. Not a single Nez Perce had died.

So began the Nez Perce War of 1877—the Nez Perce's 1,700-mile running battle against U.S. forces that General William Tecumseh Sherman later termed "one of the most extraordinary Indian wars of which there is any record."[4]

Chief Joseph's band, 1877

The united nontreaty Nez Perce bands consisted of about 300 warriors and 500 women, children, elderly, and ill people. They fled eastward with all their belongings and a large horse herd to seek safety from the soldiers. In response to Perry's humiliating loss at White Bird Canyon, General Howard took the field himself with a cavalry-infantry force of over 400 troops. The one-armed general caught up with the fleeing Indians at their camp on the south fork of the Clearwater River on July 11.

General Oliver O. Howard

Howard prematurely opened with an artillery barrage and lost any chance at surprise. A vigorous action ensued that lasted for two days. Howard finally drove the Indians from the field in a decisive victory in the Battle of Clearwater. The war might have ended right then and there, but Howard failed to pursue the fleeing Indians promptly.

On July 15, Chief Joseph and other tribal leaders held council on the Weippe Prairie. They jointly decided to trek across the Bitterroot Mountains to the plains of Montana. They hoped to find safety there among the friendly Crows. Their flight took them up the winding Lolo Trail, over the Bitterroot Mountains, across the Bitterroot Valley, and over the Continental Divide. Thinking Howard's forces trailed far behind them, they paused to rest at Montana's Big Hole River. Their pause allowed Colonel John Gibbon and a column of nearly 200 infantrymen from Fort Shaw to catch up with them.

Gibbon attacked at daybreak on August 9, surprising the Indians in their tepees and cutting down at least 89. The Battle of Big Hole raged on for two days. Rallying and counterattacking, the Nez Perce killed 29 of their attackers and wounded 40 more, including Gibbon. "The battleground was a hellish scene of devastation," writes author Kevin

Carson, "with the dead and wounded lying over the entire field."[5] The soldiers limped back to their station, and the Indians fled southeastward.

General Howard's column of 700 trailed behind the fleeing Indians, never quite catching up with their quarry. At Camas Creek (or Meadow) in Idaho, the Nez Perce skirmished with advance elements of Howard's First and Second Cavalry on August 20. Nez Perce warriors killed one trooper and wounded seven more before fleeing across the newly opened Yellowstone National Park.

Turning northeastward, Nez Perce warriors clashed with elements of the Seventh Cavalry at Canyon Creek in Montana on September 13, leaving three troopers dead and 11 wounded. Their hopes of finding safety with the friendly Crows were crushed when they found Crow scouts fighting against them as army scouts. Chief Joseph and the other Nez Perce chiefs jointly decided to make a run for Canada, which lay 200 miles to the north. Sitting Bull and the Sioux, they hoped, would welcome them as brothers.

On September 30, the Nez Perce arrived at the northern edge of the Bear Paw Mountains. Chief Looking Glass of the Alpowai band urged another pause to rest their exhausted people. Thinking again that the soldiers lagged far behind, they camped on Snake Creek, about 40 miles from Canada. But Colonel Nelson A. Miles and a garrison of troopers from Fort Keogh, Wyoming, were rushing northwestward to cut them off.

The long flight of Chief Joseph and the Nez Perce was nearing an end—but they had one last battle to fight.

Bear Paw Mountain area

"From Where the Sun Now Stands"

The last fight of the Nez Perce began on September 30, 1877. It ended six snowy and miserable days later on October 5. Colonel Nelson A. Miles attacked their camp shortly after dawn with elements of the Second and Seventh Cavalry, backed by companies of the First and Fifth Infantry.

Nez Perce warriors scrambled into positions in a cut-bank south and east of their camp. The Second Cavalry circled to the west, and the First Cavalry attacked frontally into a blizzard of fire from Indian sharpshooters. Miles called off the attack and settled into a siege. Random fighting continued over the next few days. General Howard brought up his forces but generously left Miles in command of the siege.

Chiefs Joseph, White Bird, and Looking Glass held council. Toolhoolhoolzote was dead, as was Ollokot, Joseph's younger brother and war leader. Joseph urged surrender. On October 5, Joseph faced Howard and Miles and delivered this memorable message:

> I am tired of fighting. Our chiefs are killed. . . . The old men are all dead. . . . The little children are freezing to death. . . . Hear me, my chiefs! I am tired; my heart is sick and sad. From where the sun now stands I will fight no more forever.[6]

Chief Joseph's surrender ended the Nez Perce War of 1877 and the epic journey of his people. In three months, 800 Nez Perce had traveled more than 1,700 miles across incredibly rough terrain, fighting much of the time. Around 120 of them died during the trek.

Artist Howard Terpning's painting titled, *Chief Joseph Rides to Surrender*, vividly depicts the suffering of the Nez Perce on their wintry flight across country.

CHAPTER 5
BETRAYAL AND RENEWAL:
THE NEZ PERCE TODAY

As part of the surrender terms at Bear Paw, Colonel (later General) Nelson A. Miles promised Chief Joseph that the Nez Perce would be allowed to return to their homelands. That did not happen. Instead, government bureaucrats sent them first to Kansas, and then to Indian Territory in present-day Oklahoma. "We expected to return to our homes. That was promised us by General Miles," said Yellow Wolf, Joseph's second cousin, after the Nez Perce surrendered. "That was how he got our rifles from us. It was the only way he could get them."[1]

Chief Joseph affirmed Yellow Wolf's words later: "General Miles had promised that we might return to our country with what stock we had left. . . . I believed General Miles, or I never would have surrendered."[2]

The army's two top generals, William T. Sherman and Philip H. Sheridan, later denied Miles's promise. They both agreed that neither General Howard nor Colonel Miles had the authority to make promises to prisoners. Miles, to his credit, tried for years afterward to help the Nez Perce return home, but the government continued its betrayal of his surrender terms.

The grim expressions on the faces of Chief Joseph and his family perhaps reflect their unhappiness at being exiled to Fort Leavenworth. and Indian Territory from 1877 to 1885.

"After Joseph's surrender, the United States shipped the band south to a malarial bottomland near Fort Leavenworth in eastern Kansas," writes author Alvin M. Josephy, Jr., "then to a hot, disease-ridden reservation in the Indian Territory. In both places, many of the Nez Perce who had survived the war died of sickness."[3] During this time, Joseph worked tirelessly for the right to return to the Nez Perce homeland.

In 1885, the government finally allowed Joseph and his people to return to the Northwest—but not to their homeland in Wallowa Valley (Oregon). Instead, they were sent under military escort to the Colville Reservation in Washington Territory. There they were dumped among non–Nez Perce Indians. Joseph continued to work for their return to their homeland until his death in 1904.

Today, the Nez Perce are scattered all over the world. About two-thirds of the 3,300 tribal members reside on or near the 750,000-acre Nez Perce Reservation in Idaho, with headquarters at Lapwai. Some live on the Umatilla Reservation in Oregon. Others live in various urban areas where better employment opportunities exist. Chief Joseph's band now belongs to the Confederated Tribes of the Colville Reservation, near Nespelem, Washington.

On the reservation, a council of nine members forms the governing board and oversees and directs many aspects of tribal life, including the use of natural resources and the investment of tribal income. In recent times, Nez Perce have actively pursued fishing and water rights in the Columbia River Basin. They have taken numerous steps to revitalize salmon and steelhead runs in the region. As stewards of their cherished

The Columbia Basin covers the southeastern part of the Canadian province of British Columbia, most of Idaho, Oregon, and Washington, the western part of Montana, and tiny portions of Nevada, Utah, and Wyoming.

homeland, they continue to negotiate for water rights to the Snake River and to regain ancestral lands.

In 1996, they regained 10,000 acres of their homeland in northeastern Oregon and managed the land as a wildlife preserve. Later acquisitions have increased its acreage to over 16,000. The preserve is now known as the Precious Lands Wildlife Area. It provides sanctuary for bighorn sheep, elk, cougar, salmon, and the endangered steelhead trout.

Although the Nez Perce's way of life has changed over the two centuries since their first meeting with Lewis and Clark, family traditions remain about the same. They still practice longstanding tribal rituals, and they still speak the Nez Perce language. At the same time, they have readily adapted to the changing lifestyles and technology of the twenty-first century.

This "motoring" family symbolizes the long and difficult journey of the Nez Perce—from their ancient culture to the modern age.

Nez Perce authors and storytellers visit schools like this one to tell the stories about their cultural heritage.

The Nez Perce have embraced the educational system of the United States. They provide the basic K–12 curriculum, with an emphasis on vocational training. Many of them go on to earn college degrees in medicine, engineering, journalism, teaching, and other disciplines at the University of Idaho, Washington State University, the University of Washington, and other academic institutions. Many return to the reservation to serve in such fields as wildlife management and administration.

Today, Nez Perce live in modern homes, apartments, and condominiums, though they still may use the venerable and portable tepee on camping and travel outings. For the most part, they wear modern clothes, usually purchased in stores. At ceremonies, memorials, and other special events, however, they still wear traditional garb. As in times long past, deer, elk, and salmon remain important foods for the Nez Perce, but they have also added canned foods, microwavable dishes, and TV dinners to their long-established staples. Though there are no hospitals on the Nez Perce Reservation, a health clinic at Lapwai and another at Kamiah serve the medical needs of its members.

The employment rate on the reservation is much higher than that of most other Native American tribes. Career opportunities for men include forestry, fishing and hunting, horse breeding, public administration, construction, arts, entertainment, recreation, healthcare, and social services. Career opportunities for women include public administration, arts, entertainment, recreation, educational services, healthcare, social services, retail services, and accommodation and food services. In 1995, the Nez Perce ventured into gaming, opening a casino in Kamiah. A second was opened east of Lewiston the following year. Together, the two casinos and a growing tourist trade produce a generous source of income for the tribe. In Lewiston, the heritage of the Nez Perce is celebrated in museums and historical parks as well as in the casinos.

Perhaps the most treasured profession shared by all Nez Perce is the stewardship of their beloved homelands. Their revered Chief Joseph once said, "I love that land more than all the rest of the world."[4] In his abiding spirit, today's Nez Perce continue to nourish and restore the lands where the bones of their ancestors are buried.

A new generation of Nez Perce tours the wind-swept Bear Paw Battlefield, near Chinook, Montana, among the whispering spirits of their noble ancestors.

Two Chiefs Named Joseph

History books seldom address the subject of the Nez Perce without mentioning Joseph the Younger. He is generally referred to as Chief Joseph. His prominence in the ancestral heritage of the Nez Perce is understandable and well-deserved. But there is also a *second* Chief Joseph—Joseph the Elder—who is less well-known but, arguably, equally deserving of historical acclaim.

Old Joseph

Joseph the Elder, also known as Tuekakas or Old Joseph, was the father of Young Joseph. Old Joseph served as chief of the Wallowa band of Nez Perce from 1836 until his death in 1871. In 1839, he became one of the first Nez Perce to convert to Christianity.

In 1863, following a gold rush in Wallowa country, the U. S. government reduced the size of the reservation agreed to in the Treaty of 1855 by more than ninety percent. Angered by the government's betrayal, Old Joseph slashed the American flag, shredded his Bible, and refused to sign or recognize the Treaty of 1863. He also refused to leave the Wallowa Valley. As a result, his band became one of the treaty holdouts, or nontreaty Indians. Over the next eight years, he foresaw the white man's wrongful seizure of Indian lands. Sensing his own death in 1871, he told Young Joseph, "My son, remember my dying words. This country holds your father's body. Never sell the bones of your father and mother."[5]

Young Joseph, thereafter known as Chief Joseph, honored his father's wishes, saying, "A man who would not love his father's grave is worse than a wild animal."[6]

1. The Nez Perce were once the largest congregation of tribes in the western United States.

2. Anthropologists classify the Nez Perce under two geographic divisions: Upper Nez Perce and Lower Nez Perce.

3. The Upper Nez Perce lived in the Salmon River country in Idaho and also in the Grande Ronde Valley in eastern Oregon.

4. The Lower Nez Perce inhabited the region to the north and west of Oregon's Blue Mountains on several branches of the Snake River.

5. At one point, there were over 50 bands of Nez Perce.

6. Nez Perce bands were often named after their chiefs or places of residence.

7. The Nez Perce became the only Native Americans to selectively breed their horses. They never called their horses Appaloosas. The name derives either from the Palouse River or from the Palouse tribe.

8. Congress passed laws giving the Nez Perce and other tribes status as sovereign governments.

9. Today, the U.S. Department of Agriculture Forest Service manages much of the Nez Perce tribe's lands.

10. Nez Perce people still maintain strong ties with their homeland and work cooperatively with the Forest Service as stewards of their precious forest resources.

Chapter 1. Incident at White Bird Canyon: A Brief History

1. Kevin Carson, *The Long Journey of the Nez Perce: A Battle History from Cottonwood to Bear Paw* (Yardley, PA: Westholme Publishing, 2011), p. 38.

2. David Lavender, *Let Me Be Free: The Nez Perce Tragedy* (Norman, OK: University of Oklahoma Press, 1999), p. 206.

3. Carson, p. 43.

4. Meriwether Lewis and William Clark, *The History of the Lewis and Clark Expedition,* Volume II, edited by Elliott Coues (New York: Dover Publications, 1893, n.d. reprint), p. 623.

Chapter 2. One with the Earth: The Land and Its People

1. Robert M. Utley, *The Indian Frontier of the American West 1846–1890* (Albuquerque: University of New Mexico Press, 1993), p. 7.

2. Ibid., p. 6.

3. Allen Slickpoo, "Nez Perce," in *Encyclopedia of North American Indians,* edited by Frederick E. Hoxie (Boston: Houghton Mifflin Company, 1996), p. 431.

4. David Lavender, *Let Me Be Free: The Nez Perce Tragedy* (Norman, OK: University of Oklahoma Press, 1999), p. 13.

5. Bernard DeVoto (editor), *The Journals of Lewis and Clark* (Boston: Houghton Mifflin Company, 1953), p. 323.

6. Lavender, p. 21.

Chapter 3. Religion, Spirits, and Stories

1. Robert M. Utley, *The Indian Frontier of the American West 1846–1890* (Albuquerque: University of New Mexico Press, 1993), p. 7.

2. David Lavender, *Let Me Be Free: The Nez Perce Tragedy* (Norman, OK: University of Oklahoma Press, 1999), p. 18.

3. Ibid.

4. Christopher L. Miller, "Smohalla," in *Encyclopedia of North American Indians,* edited by Frederick E. Hoxie (Boston: Houghton Mifflin Company, 1996), p. 601.

5. Ibid.

Chapter 4. Chief Joseph and the Long Flight

1. Alvin M. Josephy, Jr., *500 Nations: An Illustrated History of North American Indians* (New York: Alfred A. Knopf, 1994), p. 414.

2. Kevin Carson, *The Long Journey of the Nez Perce: A Battle History from Cottonwood to Bear Paw* (Yardley, PA: Westholme Publishing, 2011), p. 44.

3. Ibid.

4. Josephy, p. 414.

5. Carson, p. 154.

6. Alan Axelrod, *Chronicle of the Indian Wars: From Colonial Times to Wounded Knee* (New York: Prentice Hall General Reference, 1993), p. 235.

Chapter 5. Betrayal and Renewal: The Nez Perce Today

1. David Lavender, *Let Me Be Free: The Nez Perce Tragedy* (Norman, OK: University of Oklahoma Press, 1999), p. 325.

2. Ibid.

3. Alvin M. Josephy, Jr., *500 Nations: An Illustrated History of North American Indians* (New York: Alfred A. Knopf, 1994), p. 417.

4. Ibid., p. 412.

5. Lavender, p. 196.

6. Josephy, p. 412.

Bear Paw battlefield

Books

Bonvillain, Nancy. *The Nez Perce.* The History and Culture of Native Americans Series. New York: Chelsea House Publishers, 2010.

Bradley, Kathleen E. *Chief Joseph and the Nez Perce: Expanding and Preserving the Union.* Reader's Theater Series. Huntington Beach, CA: Shell Educational Publishing, 2009.

Dwyer, Helen. *Nez Perce History and Culture.* Native American Library Series. New York: Gareth Stevens Publishing, 2012.

Englar, Mary. *Chief Joseph, 1840–1904.* American Indian Biography Series. Mankato, MN: Capstone Press, 2004.

King, David C. *The Nez Perce.* First Americans Series. Tarrytown, NY: Marshall Cavendish, 2007.

Works Consulted

Axelrod, Alan. *Chronicle of the Indian Wars: From Colonial Times to Wounded Knee.* New York: Prentice Hall General Reference, 1993.

Bakeless, John. *Lewis and Clark: Partners in Discovery.* Mineola, NY: Dover Publications, 1996.

Carson, Kevin. *The Long Journey of the Nez Perce: A Battle History from Cottonwood to Bear Paw.* Yardley, PA: Westholme Publishing, 2011.

DeVoto, Bernard, editor. *The Journals of Lewis and Clark.* The American Heritage Library. Boston: Houghton Mifflin Company, 1953.

Furtwangler, Albert. *Acts of Discovery: Visions of America in the Lewis and Clark Journals.* Chicago: University of Illinois, 1993.

Grant, Bruce. Concise *Encyclopedia of the American Indian.* Rev. ed. New York: Wings Books, 1994.

Greene, Jerome. *Nez Perce Summer 1877: The U.S. Army and the Nee-Me-Poo Crisis.* Big Hole National Battlefield. http://www.nps.gov/history/history/online_books/nepe/greene/index.htm

Hirschfelder, Arlene, and Paulette Molin. *The Encyclopedia of Native American Religions.* New York: MJF Books, 1992.

Hoxie, Frederick E., editor. *Encyclopedia of North American Indians.* Boston: Houghton Mifflin Company, 1996.

Josephy, Alvin M., Jr. *500 Nations: An Illustrated History of North American Indians.* New York: Alfred A. Knopf, 1994.

Lavender, David. *Let Me Be Free: The Nez Perce Tragedy.* Norman, OK: University of Oklahoma Press, 1999.

Lewis, Meriwether, and William Clark. *The History of the Lewis and Clark Expedition.* Volumes I–III. 1893. Reprint. Edited by Elliott Coues. New York: Dover Publications, n.d.

Mails, Thomas E. *The Mystic Warriors of the Plains.* New York: Perseus Books Group, 2002.

Milner, Clyde A., II, Carol A. O'Connor, and Martha A. Sandweiss, editors. *The Oxford History of the American West.* New York: Oxford University Press, 1994.

Nerburn, Kent. *Chief Joseph & the Flight of the Nez Perce: The Untold Story of an American Tragedy.* New York: HarperCollins Publishers, 2006.

Terrell, John Upton. *American Indian Almanac.* New York: Barnes & Noble Books, 1994.

Thomas, David Hurst, Jay Miller, Richard White, Peter Nabokov, and Philip J. Deloria. *The Native Americans: An Illustrated History.* Atlanta: Turner Publishing, 1993.

Utley, Robert M. *The Indian Frontier of the American West 1846–1890.* Albuquerque: University of New Mexico Press, 1993.

Utley, Robert M., and Wilcomb E. Washburn. *The American Heritage History of the Indian Wars.* New York: Barnes & Noble Books, 1992.

On the Internet

Countries and Their Cultures: Nez Perce
http://www.everyculture.com/multi/Le-Pa/Nez-Perc.html

Native American Facts for Kids: Nez Perce Tribe
http://www.bigorrin.org/nez_kids.htm

Nez Perce History
http://www.nezperce.org/History/MainHistory.html

PBS: Lewis and Clark, Nez Perce Indians
http://www.pbs.org/lewisandclark/native/nez.html

anthropologist (an-throh-PALL-uh-jist)—A scientist who studies human beings, especially in relation to distribution, origin, classification, and relationship of races, physical character, environmental and social relations, and culture.

bureaucrat (BYOOR-uh-krat)—A government official.

camas (KAH-mus)—Plants of the lily family with edible roots; found chiefly in the western United States.

Dreamer Religion—A religious revitalization movement of Plateau Indians. In the 1850s, the Wanapam shaman Smohalla claimed he had visited the Spirit World and had returned to preach the resurgence of their original way of life, free from white influences such as alcohol and agriculture.

expansionism (ek-SPAN-shuh-nizm)—A policy or theory of expansion.

firewater—Whiskey (slang).

malarial (muh LAYR-ee-ul)—Of or related to the disease of malaria.

Penutian (puh-NOO-tee-en)—A superfamily of North American Indian languages that includes languages mainly of the far western United States and Canada.

Sahaptin (suh-HAP-ten)—A member of a group of American Indian peoples who formerly inhabited a large territory along the Columbia River and its tributaries; the language of the Sahaptin people including Nez Perce and Yakima.

shaman (SHAH-mun)—A mediator between the world of spirits and that of humans and animals; a tribal member who interprets and attempts to control the supernatural, using his powers to bring success in food gathering and warfare and to cure the sick.

siege (SEEDJ)—The surrounding or blockading of a town or fortress by armed forces.

vocational (voh-KAY-shun-ul)—Of or related to a trade or profession.

wyakin (wye-YEK-en)—A guardian spirit; an occult force that forms a part of Native American spirituality; a word specific to the Nez Perce language.

MEET THE
AUTHOR

Earle Rice Jr. is a former senior design engineer and technical writer in the aerospace, electronic-defense, and nuclear industries. He has been a full-time writer since 1993 and is author of over 70 published books. Rice is listed in *Who's Who in America* and is a member of the Society of Children's Book Writers and Illustrators, the League of World War I Aviation Historians, the Air Force Association, and the Disabled American Veterans.